SCARBOROUGH
A Pictorial History

Newborough Bar, 1890.

SCARBOROUGH
A Pictorial History

R. J. Percy

Phillimore

1995

Published by
PHILLIMORE & CO. LTD.,
Shopwyke Manor Barn, Chichester, West Sussex

ISBN 0 85033 954 5

Printed and bound in Great Britain by
BIDDLES LTD.
Guildford, Surrey

For my Mother and Father

List of Illustrations

Frontispiece: Newborough Bar, 1896

Acknowledgements

I am indebted to Mr. Neil Speight and his staff at *Yorkshire Regional Newspapers Ltd.*, for the help they have given me by allowing me the use of their archives. I would also like to thank Bryan Berryman, Georgie England, Anne Mitchell and Colin Storry for bearing with me.

I would like to thank the following for the use of the following illustrations: Nora Benson, 49; Les Day, 4, 10, 17, 113-15; Georgie England, 40; Miss Hatfield, 163; Ted Hunt, 96; Mr. and Mrs. Lyth, 33; Edward Midgley, 28, 69-70, 78, 117-18, 124, 131, 141, 147, 165, 167, 176; Minnie Midgley, 154; Anne Mitchell, 11, 13, 16-8, 25, 35, 41, 55, 59, 72, 80, 135, 151, 155-6, 162, 167; Frances and James Percy, 41, 46, 55-6, 112, 150-1, 157-60; George Pottage, 76; Gordon Pottage, 59; The University of Reading, Museum of English Rural Life, 42; Mary Riby, 116; David Stokes, 87, 134; Margaret Willis, 115, 178; *Yorkshire Regional Newspapers Ltd.*, 99-111. The rest of the illustrations are from the author's own collection.

Introduction

Scarborough stands in a unique position on the Yorkshire coast with unparalleled views to the north and south. She also has a rich and varied history.

There are various theories about when the town was founded, and by whom. However, the Romans who established a signal station on what is now called Castle Hill in the year 350 can be ruled out as they only manned the station with a token force and were only there for a period of about 50 years.

The most widely accepted view is that the Icelandic Viking, Thorgills Skaroi, or as it is more commonly written, Skarthi, founded a settlement in or around the year 966. The name Skaroi is a nickname meaning 'hare lip' and in old manuscripts we see references to Scardeburc, Scartheburg and Scaroeborc, all pointers to possible Scandinavian influence.

Surprisingly, Scarborough is not mentioned in Domesday Book. Compiled in 1086, the purpose of this book was to gather information regarding the value of crown lands, the levying of land tax and other dues and to discover the wealth of the barons. The most probable reason for the town being omitted are the events that occurred 20 years earlier.

In 1066 Harold Hardrada, King of Norway, formed an alliance with Tostig, Earl of Falsgrave and brother to the English king, Harold. He gathered a force of warriors and sailed for the British Isles, landing at the Shetlands where he was joined by Tostig. They set sail and arrived at Scarborough where they waded ashore and with Nordic battle cries burned and pillaged the small settlement.

We are lucky that Thorklein, a northern historian, describes the scene in one of his essays:

> Sithence he lay to at Scarborough and fought with the burghermen; he ascended the hill which is there, and caused a great pyre to be made there, and set on fire. When the fire spread, they took great forks and threw the brands on the town; and when one house took fire from another, they gave up all the town. The Northmen slew many people, and seized all that they found.

It would appear by his account that the damage done to the settlement was so severe that there simply was nothing left worth recording, although it is interesting to note that Walsgrave (now Falsgrave) and the hamlet of Northstead, which today form part of the borough, are mentioned in Domesday Book.

It was well into the 12th century before the town recovered from this onslaught. This was due entirely to its geographical feature, the lofty promontory rising to 300 ft. above sea level which was thought to be totally inaccessible.

In the reign of King Stephen, about the year 1136, a nobleman of Norman extraction, William le Gros, Earl of Albemarle and Holderness, sought permission of the king to build a castle at Scarborough. His wish was granted and he went ahead with the project which proved to be a costly venture. Nevertheless, the end result was what was described at the time as 'a great and noble castle'. Noble it might have been, but within 70 years it had fallen into disrepair and it was well into the reign of Henry II before it was restored to its former grandeur.

By the year 1265 Scarborough had become a thriving and prosperous sea port. Pirates were always a threat as they lurked out at sea waiting for the town's fishermen to sail. This led to boats being manned with armed men but it was well into the 18th century before this problem was overcome.

The Vikings are reputed to have built the first pier at Scarborough. It would have been a very primitive structure, suitable for their needs but of little use to a busy harbour. Over the years, from about 1252 onwards, various monarchs made grants towards the upkeep of the harbour as they recognised its importance as a naval base sheltering as it did under the castle's guns.

During the war against France in 1542 the port went into a decline. This was due to the fact that Scarborough had no armed ships to protect her commerce. Obviously the guns along the castle walls were no deterrent and this became evident when three Scottish men-of-war anchored in the bay and, by simply having sufficient fire power, commanded all shipping in the area.

With the cessation of hostilities Scarborough once again looked to the future. An Act of Parliament was passed in 1546 imposing a duty on the pier. Initially, all was well but, either through bad workmanship or the elements, within 20 years the pier was in such a dilapidated state that an appeal was made to Elizabeth I to grant money for the essential work to be carried out.

The queen was generous and vast improvements were made. However, it was not until the reign of George II that any real effort was made to create a harbour that had all the necessary requirements needed to cater for the many vessels that were expected to use the port.

By 1752 the Inner (Vincents) Pier had been completed. In the early 19th century the authorities engaged William Smeaton of Eddystone Lighthouse fame to design the East Pier. This pier took over 50 years to complete at a cost of £12,000. The stone slabs each weighing 30 tons were quarried locally and convicts were employed on the job. The West Pier was built shortly afterwards using the stones from the little-used Island Pier.

Whether there was a lighthouse at Scarborough prior to 1804 is not known. It was in that year that the first recording of such a building was made. This primitive, flat-roofed structure was situated on Vincent's Pier and its only light was from a brazier that stood on the top of it. In 1850 the lighthouse had another storey added and firstly candles, then oil and gas, and finally electricity were used to throw the beam out to sea.

As one century passed into the next, life in Scarborough began to change considerably. Whereas the castle had been the centrepoint of the town, guarding the small fishing and trading port sheltering under its walls, by the 17th century its influence had waned into insignificance. The change came about by a chance discovery made by a respectable Scarborough lady. In 1626 Mistress Farrar noticed one day, when walking along the sands, that the stones were tinged a strange, brownish-red colour where water trickled out of the ground. After sampling the water she carried out a series of experiments and declared with glee that it had curative properties.

Suddenly, the name of Scarborough was echoing around all the best salons in the country. The nobility and landed gentry avoided their usual summer haunts and with their entourage of servants set off in their carriages to what had become known as the 'Queen of Watering Places'.

The Spaw (the usual spelling in the 17th and 18th centuries) waters were said to cure

diseases of the head, cleanse the stomach, opens the lungs, cures asthma and scurvy, purifies the blood, it cures the jaunders both yellow and black, the leprosie and is the most sovereign remedy against Hypochondriak Melancholly and Windiness.

With such wondrous beneficial qualities it is no surprise that the celebrated Spa traveller, Dr. Granville, stated in rapturous tones, 'Scarborough is one of the most interesting marine Spas in England'.

The Corporation who owned the land where the springs came out of the ground were quick to realise its commercial value. They erected a primitive wood hut which they manned with old women who, armed with long sticks with attached cups, reached down into the wells and filled drinking horns with the iron-tasting water.

The customers became ecstatic over the health-giving waters. One visitor, Mark Hildesley, Bishop of Sodor and Man, enjoyed a daily glass but, by the time he had climbed back up the hill, he exclaimed exhaustively, the good effects had left him.

In 1737 an earthquake occurred at Scarborough which not only shook the old Spaw House so much that it collapsed in a heap, it also brought down part of the cliff containing about an acre of pasture land. If this was not calamitous enough, the Spaw water ceased running. It could have meant ruination for the town. Professional men were quickly brought in and after a painstaking search which involved clearing away tons of mud, the springs suddenly gushed out of the ground. Two years later a new Spaw House was built.

In 1826 a number of influential men from York and Scarborough formed the Cliff Bridge Company. Their main aim was to develop the Spa (note the change in spelling). They obtained a 99-year lease on the Corporation-owned land around the Spa and raised over £4,000 to construct a bridge that would provide easy access from the town to the wells. The new Cliff Bridge opened to much jubilation on 19 July 1827.

Seven years later a storm badly damaged the wooden Spa House and the Cliff Bridge Company took the opportunity to negotiate a 200-year lease for the site. The architect Henry Wyatt was commissioned to design a building and in 1839 his stone Gothic saloon opened. The original Pump Room with the famous water took second place to the Saloon which provided music and entertainment.

In 1857 the eminent architect Sir Joseph Paxton took an interest in the Spa and submitted plans for more extensive buildings and landscaping of the grounds. His ideas pleased the company and by 1860 a carriageway had been constructed, the promenade lengthened, the Grand Hall built and Italinate terraces led up into well laid out gardens.

Tragedy struck in 1876 at a time when the Grand Hall was being used as a bazaar in aid of St Mary's Parish Church Fund. A fire broke out which completely destroyed Paxton's masterpiece. Undeterred, the Corporation commissioned two architects Verity and Hunt to design a suitable building. There arose the magnificent hall that one sees today and which was opened with civic splendour by the Lord Mayor of London in 1880.

By the mid-18th century the population of Scarborough numbered only 8,000 inhabitants, whose main occupation was fishing and boat building. The town had not expanded beyond the lines laid down three centuries before.

It became evident that Scarborough was no longer the first-class port she had once been and all energy was now concentrated on developing the tourist trade. Elegant lodging houses were built on St Nicholas Cliff and Long Room Street (now St Nicholas Street) which became known as the 'Pall Mall' of Scarborough. Anybody who was anybody had to be seen there promenading in fine clothes before visiting the Long Room itself. This establishment was kept by Mon. Vipont, master of the Long Room at Hampstead. He spared no expense in giving his customers what they wanted. Cooks were brought up from London and everything was conducted in the 'politest manner'. There was a music gallery where the ladies could gather and in the adjoining rooms the gentlemen could gamble to their hearts' content at the Pharo banks, hazard tables and fair chance.

On 7 July 1845 the engines *Hudson* and *Lyon* drew a train of 35 first-class carriages to Scarborough to celebrate the opening of the York to Scarborough railway. The journey took three and a quarter hours, passing through various stations where bunting fluttered in the breeze and locals watched in sheer disbelief at this revolutionary mode of transport. Until that date the only main route into town from the West Riding had been along the old turnpike road which ran via Malton and Snainton. Although it was not realised at the time, the railways were to change the face of the country forever. The future of Scarborough's coaches with such nostalgic names as 'Old True Blue', 'Wellington', 'Royal Union', 'British Queen', 'Prince Blucher', 'Regulator', 'Express', 'High Flyer' and 'Safety' which ran from the principal inns looked bleak and their days were numbered.

The taking of the Spa waters lost its appeal, resulting in a steady decline of the affluent classes but, thanks to the railway, visitors from different backgrounds converged upon the town. They were not interested one little bit in the healing power of the water. It was the sea, the sand, the rides on the donkeys and the ice-cream parlours that attracted them.

The town was not really geared for this onslaught and a development programme was put in hand. Large hotels such as the *Grand* and the *Pavilion* were built and along the North Cliff boarding houses rose at an alarming rate.

The foreshore, until then a maze of mast yards and fish storing sheds, was redesigned. Many of the old buildings were completely demolished and in their place were erected cafés and souvenir shops. So confident were the powers-that-be that in 1856 a new road, Eastborough, was bulldozed through the old town giving greater access to the harbour and beach.

The population of Scarborough grew in leaps and bounds. By 1851 there were about 13,000 inhabitants; by 1891 the number had risen to a staggering 33,000!

New suburbs sprang up connecting the village of Falsgrave to the town. What had once been green fields were now streets of neat terrace houses and well laid out squares with villas for the middle-classes. The future looked assured and Scarborough felt confident knowing that she was indeed 'Queen of the Yorkshire Coast'.

As the 20th century drew near, the transformation of the town from a flourishing shipbuilding port to seaside resort was nearly complete. However, ships still played a minor rôle in the carriage of merchandise and people to places such as London and Sunderland, and even as late as the 1920s the ship *Scarborough* was plying this route.

Transport in town was another matter. The Sedan chair had arrived from London in the mid-18th century but it was 1836 before the first cab was to be seen in the streets of Scarborough. By the turn of the century there were over 200 horse-drawn cabs and landaus for hire. After the First World War this mode of transport was forced out of business by the electric tram, omnibus and motor car. By 1936 only 20 cabs remained in town.

The early years of the 20th century saw Scarborough basking in her glory as the premier seaside resort on the east coast. The hotels and boarding houses were crowded with the middle-class holiday maker who had replaced the landed gentry. The town could offer a wide range of entertainment. The famous Will Catlin's Pierrots were on the south sands, at the newly opened Floral Hall the Fol-de-Rols were playing to full houses and for those

1 An aerial view of the South Sands in 1935.

wishing culture The Theatre Royal (whose royal patron was no other than Prince of Wales), the Grand Opera House and the Londesborough Theatre were all staging the classics.

On 4 August 1914 Great Britain declared war upon Germany. Initially, one would have been forgiven for thinking that the country was still at peace. There was no panic-stricken departure by the visitors, the only sign of war being the queues of young men at Army recruitment centres. Why should anyone panic, visitor and local alike felt completely safe knowing that the Royal Navy, the mightiest in the world, was not only guardian of the Empire but of the shores of Britain herself.

An event on Wednesday, 16 December 1914 sent shock waves through the British Isles. At 8 a.m. on that fateful day a grey fog clung to the coast obscuring visibility. Slowly and silently the menacing silhouettes of two German battle cruisers, the *Derrflinger* and the *Von Der Tann*, accompanied by the light cruiser, *Kolberg*, steamed into full view and closed to within one mile of the resort. The smaller ship made off in a southerly direction laying mines as she went. The two remaining battle cruisers trained their 11- and 12-inch guns on the ancient battlements of the castle where the gunners knew the Admiralty Signal Station was situated. An accurate salvo reduced the building to rubble. The Germans were reluctant to move in closer to the shore as they were under the impression that Scarborough was a fortified town. In actual fact the only armaments were four rusty 18th-century cannon that stood in the castle yard. Seeing that there was no answering fire the ships closed in and with a mighty roar opened up a steady fire upon the peaceful town.

The bombardment lasted about half an hour and within that time over 520 shells had exploded resulting in the deaths of 18 people including eight women and four children. Over 210 buildings suffered varying degrees of damage. Churches were struck and the *Grand Hotel* and *Royal* suffered severely. The Town Hall, Workhouse, Gladstone Road school and the Hospital all shuddered under the impact of direct hits.

Panic suddenly set in and people ran out into the street shouting that the Germans were coming. Whole families made their way into the outlying villages; some just wandered about in a daze.

A message was telegraphed to York where the 8th West Yorkshire Regiment was billeted. They quickly mobilised and arrived in Scarborough at 2.30 p.m. where they positioned themselves at strategic points throughout the town. This military show of strength was all in vain. By that time the enemy ships were safely back in home waters after successfully evading Beatty's squadron which had steamed to intercept them.

We now know that the Admiralty knew of this attack well in advance but dared not send warships as they feared the Germans would realise that their codes had been broken.

Slowly the residents of Scarborough returned home but there was always the dread of another attack. As the months and years passed by their fears lessened. There was still the Zeppelin to contend with but, even though their steady drone overhead made peoples' hearts pound that bit quicker, no bombs fell on Scarborough itself; the nearest landed at Seamer some three miles away. Then, on 6 September 1917 their deep-rooted fears materialised. At 6.45 p.m. on a beautiful sunny evening when the Foreshore was crowded with locals and a few visitors who had braved wartime travel, an enemy U-boat surfaced four miles off the resort. It lay there for 15 minutes before opening fire. Thirty rounds were fired at the town. Half of the shells fell among fishing and pleasure boats in the bay causing no noticeable damage. The other half smashed into buildings and caused the deaths of three people and injuring another five. Ironically, minesweepers laying at anchor in the bay had chosen to ignore the submarine until it was too late. Although they raised steam and set off in pursuit, the enemy vessel had submerged and made its escape.

On 11 November 1918, the Prime Minister announced to cheering crowds that the Armistice had been signed and that all hostilities would cease at 11 a.m. In Scarborough the news was greeted with jubilation but also with great sadness for the families of the 636 local men who up to the date were known to have been killed.

It was the following year, 19 July 1919, when the town celebrated in style. Fireworks and rockets soared into the night sky and burst over the Castle Hill. There was dancing on the Spa to Alick Maclean and his Orchestra and at 11 p.m. the celebrations came to a grand finale when the ancient beacon on the castle wall was set alight. Everyone said it was the war to end wars. The boys were arriving home and the future looked secure.

The years leading up to the Second World War witnessed large-scale redevelopment with the aim of making Scarborough a top-class modern seaside resort. The old town suffered the most in the name of progress. Street after street of fishermen's quaint cottages were demolished as were churches and public buildings. The large open sites that resulted were either grassed over or turned into car parks.

The North Side, until then a rural backwater, was made attractive to the visitor by the laying out of parks and gardens. The Miniature Railway and the Open Air Theatre (said by the Lord Mayor of London to be the best in England) were functioning by 1931 and 1932. These were followed in 1938 with the final phase of the project, the North Bay Swimming Pool.

The town expanded outwards and large estates sprang up at Edgehill, Newby and Northstead. What were once open fields connecting Scarborough to the villages of Throxenby and Scalby were now the new suburbia. By the end of the Second World War no large undeveloped areas of land could be found within the Municipal boundaries.

During the Munich crisis of 1938 when the famous piece of paper was waved confidently by Mr. Chamberlain as he declared, 'Peace in our time', gas masks were being issued to the residents of Scarborough along with everyone else in the kingdom.

By 1 September 1939, only two days before war was declared, the first batch of evacuees arrived in town from Hull, Middlesbrough and West Hartlepool. Over the following days 14,000 refugee families would be billeted in Scarborough. With the commencement of hostilities the town suddenly became a prohibited area. All roads leading into the centre were barricaded and manned by armed soldiers. The beaches, cliffs and promenades resembled a battlefield as barbed wire and mines were laid in case of an invasion.

Summer 1939 had seen the resort packed with holidaymakers. The same could not be said of 1940. The sands were bare, prohibited areas and anyone venturing onto them was a foolish person indeed. One young lady did lose her life one night when a sentry shot her after she ignored his warning. The military moved in and every boarding house, hotel and place of entertainment including the Spa and Floral Hall was requisitioned and occupied by the armed forces who remained for the duration. Scarborough's first air raid warning wailed out at 9.25 a.m. on 29 January 1940 when German planes were spotted flying over Cayton Bay. On this occasion nothing occurred but the following months saw the town subjected to tip-and-run raids which caused considerable damage to property but resulted in the deaths of only four people.

Of course this could not last. Scarborough had too many important targets, including the Admiralty's Wireless Station, barracks and harbour.

On 18 March 1941 the sirens sounded the alert at 8.10 p.m. as 98 enemy aircraft flew in over the Wolds and showered the villages of Flixton and Folkton with incendiaries. At 9 p.m. they closed in on Scarborough and subjected the town to two hours of heavy, indiscriminate bombing with high explosives, delayed action bombs, parachute mines and thousands of incendiaries. There then followed sporadic attacks when further parachute mines were dropped. The All-Clear sounded at 4.30 a.m. the following day. What became known locally as the 'March Blitz' proved a trying time for the town's war-time services. At one point during the raid the fires became so serious that the AFS had to call for assistance and appliances were rushed in from other towns.

The result of the raid was that 1,378 buildings had either been destroyed or damaged. There had been 27 fatalities—a high number when one considers the size of Scarborough—with a further 45 suffering injury. The town had to endure many more raids but never on such a large scale.

Victory in Europe Day, 8 May 1945, brought the threat of air attack to an end. The town had suffered 21 air raids and five machine gun and cannon attacks. The casualties from bombs and mines numbered 47 deaths with a further 137 suffering wounds. Over 3,000 of the town's buildings were destroyed or damaged.

Post-war planning got off to a shaky start. The build-up of the tourist trade was top priority but had to take second place until a solution to the homeless could be found. There were 2,460 applications for houses; 804 of these applicants had no home at all. A large estate was built at Sandybed in 1945 using German prisoners-of-war as labour. Another estate was laid out at Barrowcliff which eased the situation a little.

Now the holiday trade could be concentrated on. This was not as easy as it looked. The military were still in the hotels and it was well into 1947 before they de-requisitioned them. Even then it was not plain sailing. Many of the large hotels had given their furniture to the Americans to furnish their billets. There was also a shortage of soap and linen. But, by the late 1940s most of the problems had been overcome and by the start of the new decade Scarborough was once again being hailed as the Premier Resort of the East Coast.

Streets and Buildings

2 Looking from the present Mount Park Road, Falsgrave, the eye is drawn from the old 18th-century cottages to the huge block of yellow stone and brick which forms West Park Terrace. It was built in 1866 and the prime mover of the project is thought to have been Dr. Thomas T. Peirson of 52 Westborough, Scarborough.

3 A view of the same cottages taken in 1870 but from another angle. The cottages remained well into the 1920s although in a very dilapidated state. Today a private house stands on the site.

4   Quaint cottages at the junction of Scalby Road and Falsgrave Road in the 1920s capture the feel of old Falsgrave village. The entrance on the far left led into Shield's Yard. All this property has now been demolished and is the car park for a nearby public house.

5   Ivy House, Sandside, seen here in 1896, is now a restaurant, but was then a private house. It was built in the early 18th century but in recent years has had many alterations. Purnell and Son, established in 1847, is seen advertised on the board to the left.

6 Sandside in the early 1900s shows Edmond's mast yard. The alleyway on the right is still there today and is known as March's Lane and leads to the *Three Mariners Inn.*

7 The buildings on the left are all that remain of the original Sandside after work had finished to improve access to the Marine Drive.

8 St Paul's Cocoa House is advertised on the board at the corner of Castle Road and Regent Street. The foundation stone was laid by Lady Legard, the wife of Sir Charles Legard of Ganton Hall near Scarborough, in 1878 and the Cocoa House opened the following year. Cheap meals were served to the poor and eventually it was converted into a mission room. It was demolished *c*.1961.

9 This photograph taken in the late 19th century shows a scene that is unrecognisable today. The cottage and mast yard of Terry and Jennings was demolished about 1890 to make way for what became the Olympia Ballroom on Foreshore Road.

10 A view of Castlegate in 1900 shows elegant Georgian houses that at one time belonged to the town's merchant families. Much of the street was demolished when a land mine exploded nearby in Potter Lane on 10 October 1940.

11 Prince of Wales Terrace in 1904 typifies Victorian respectability. The whole of South Cliff went under the name New Scarborough when it was built from about 1845 onwards. Surprisingly, these houses were nothing more than glorified boarding houses, although if asked, the owners would reply, 'We take paying guests'.

12 Brunswick Terrace, pictured here *c.*1900, no longer exists; demolished in 1988 to make way for the Brunswick Centre. The house on the right was the birthplace of Frederick Lord Leighton (1830-98) who became President of the Royal Academy of Art and was raised to the peerage in 1896.

13 The blast-damaged Leighton House flats (once a hotel) at the corner of Brunswick Terrace and Vernon Road lay derelict after a raid in 10 May 1941, which left 150 premises damaged. Leighton House was demolished in 1946.

14 The Theatre Royal, St Thomas Street, was the town's oldest theatre, but in this picture from 1924 it lies derelict and up for sale. It had been built in 1767 and English and foreign royalty were among its patrons. The building was demolished in the late 1920s and a nightclub now stands on the site.

15 The Albert Hall was one of the town's first Liberal clubs and stood on Aberdeen Walk adjoining the Post Office. It was built in the 1870s, but on Monday, 14 July 1942 it suddenly collapsed. Luckily there were no casualties. Investigations carried out revealed that an air raid on 10 May 1941 had caused structural weakness resulting in its collapse.

16 Globe Street, seen here in 1932, was originally called Stockdale Street after the owner of the *Old Globe Inn*. In the backyard of this inn the Freemasons built their lodge in 1797. The building with the porch was the original inn which became a Model Lodging House. The street was demolished in 1934.

17 Short's Gardens was originally called Frazier's Bank but took the name from William Short who came to live here. On 10 October 1940, a landmine exploded in Potter's Lane and blasted a hole 60 ft. wide by 30 ft. deep. Over 500 houses were damaged or destroyed. The damage to Short's Gardens was so severe that it had to be demolished.

18 Lower Conduit Street in 1955. The house on the left had originally been the *Brass Tap* inn until it lost its licence in 1904. The cottage to the right dates back to the 17th century when it was Farrer's Hospital, named after John Farrer, a respected citizen of the town. Today, all has been demolished and is now known as Princess Square.

19 The demolition of Auborough Street is almost complete as this picture, taken in September 1955, shows. The large building to the right is the rear of the Old Hospital on Friar's Entry which was itself demolished a decade later.

20 Auborough Street looking from Castle Road in 1957, before the road was widened. The newly-built St Mary's Parish House, seen on the left, was erected on the site of Auborough House, the home of the Nesfield brewery family, and was said to have been the most interesting house in town.

21 Dark and mysterious Quay Street at the turn of the century had an atmosphere all of its own. It is reputed to be haunted by a coach and horses that can be heard galloping at full speed along the street. This view was taken in the 1920s and the thoroughfare still retains its character.

"OLD SCARBOROUGH."

22 & 23 Quay Street in 1935, and Dog and Duck Lane. The lane is said to have derived its name from a man living nearby who was nicknamed 'Doggy' Duck and who kept a barking dog. The old timbered building on the corner was originally the *Dog and Duck Inn*. All the property in Quay Street was demolished in the late 1930s but this building remains and forms part of the *Lancaster Inn*.

24 'Crazy Cottage', Quay Street, seen in 1962, was then only days away from being demolished. It acquired its name from the crazy angle at which it stood. For years it was the home of 'Diddy' Scales and her lodger, the man who acted the part of Long John Silver on the *Hispaniola*, on Treasure Island at the Mere (see illustration 160).

25 St Mary's Street in 1963 shows quaint cottages which had not changed in over one hundred years. They were demolished in about 1964.

26 The tower standing in the gardens of Woodend was erected as a folly by Sir George Sitwell, sometime between the years 1880-90, and was used as a cooling house for his wine. Woodend is now a museum.

27 King Richard III House, Sandside, is reputed to have been the lodging house where the king stayed when he was Lord High Admiral to his brother Edward IV in 1484. A Manchester antique dealer opened the building to the public in 1914 as a museum. After he was lost on the *Lusitania*, his partner, Mr. Burrows, took over and ran it until 1964

Trade and Industry

28 Fishermen gather on the Fish Pier, *c*.1876. The Foreshore Road was not built until the 1870s. In the background is the *Lord Nelson Hotel* and, directly behind the fishermen, the Sandside Coffee House.

29 Gullen's shop at 1 Hampton Road appears to sell just about everything from legs of ham to brushes. The view has changed little since this photograph was taken in 1892. The hay stacks have gone to be replaced by Harley Terrace, which is now known as 35-45 Scalby Road.

30 George Dale Smith's Wholesale and Retail Silk Mercers and General Drapers at 65-6 Newborough was a very high-class establishment, founded nearly 200 years ago. He took over the adjoining shop, which had to be enlarged twice, once in 1883 and then again the following year. At night the windows were lit by six electroliers—very modern indeed for the time.

31 Simeon Lord's ironmongers stood at 54 Newborough. It had orginally been the *Red Lion* public house which was kept by, amongst others, Mary Nicholson and Samuel Hardy. It later became John Westlake's ironmongers and finally in the 1930s an amusement arcade. It was demolished along with the adjoining property in 1964.

32 Ruddock's, Eccles' chemist and Stewart and Leek's bakers at 1-10 Westborough are shown here in 1895. They became Randall's, Spall's and the Maypole Dairy which many people may still remember. Today the façades are greatly altered.

33 Thirteen members of the staff of Stewart and Leek's bakers pose outside the shop, *c.*1895. In the window a mouth-watering display of newly-baked bread and confectionery can be seen. The shop obviously had a good turn-over as two horse-drawn delivery vans were needed.

34 Westborough in 1897. Most of the property between 110-15 Westborough was demolished in 1973, such as the *Balmoral Hotel*, on the far right of the picture (then known as the *Bull Hotel*) and the Bar church. The *Adelphi Hotel* which opened in the 1880s was closed to become the Adelphi Chambers in 1911. Whitfield's chemist lasted well into the 1960s before it too closed.

35 Spread Eagle Lane, in 1899, lies on the seaward side of Sandside and was a hive of tenements and mast yards until 1904 when it was demolished to make an easier access to the Marine Drive.

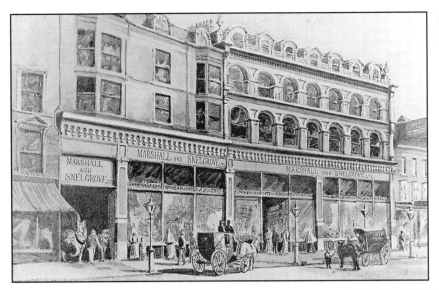

36 Marshall and Snelgrove's, St Nicholas Street, was one of the most elegant department stores in Scarborough. It opened in the 1860s and remained a high-class shopping centre until the 1970s. A doorman dressed in green livery stood on the pavement and would not allow people in unless he thought them 'suitable' customers.

37 W. C. Land and Co., South Street, was renowned for its quality foods and service. On the rich and respectable South Cliff no residents at the turn of the century would dream of being seen in the shop; they always sent their servants. The business has long gone and today South Street is no longer the thoroughfare it once was.

38 Shopkeepers, including Naomi the Palmist and Character Reader, look on in interest while a photograph of Blands Cliff is being taken in 1901. Until 1722 the only access to the beach was down Merchant's Row and West Sandgate. Mr. John Bland, a merchant, constructed Blands Cliff at his own expense.

39 Jonathan Smith, Provision Dealer, 1-2 Sandside, is being very patriotic in welcoming the Channel Fleet in 1909. These visits by the fleet were a regular event and as many as 20 warships could be seen anchored in the bay at any one time. The property is now an amusement arcade.

40 Corner shops such as this one, above left, at the junction of Roseberry Avenue and Seamer Road are almost becoming a thing of the past. The photograph was taken in about 1910. The sign reads, 'Cheapest house for stockings, aprons, corsets, see them'.

41 Dumple Street, above right, was considered by many to be the street with the most colourful characters. There was Lizzie Richardson's shop, famous for her hot cakes and bacon at 2d. a portion and Chapman's shop on the left where one could buy a bladder of lard. Dumple Street was demolished in 1930 and the new thoroughfare which replaced it took the name Friargate.

42 Court Green Farm shop, 13 Castle Road, below, was in business from 1932-37. Their products were home-grown at the family farm at Cloughton. The notice in the window explains that the milk bottles were sealed with special aluminium caps within five minutes of milking.

Roads and Transport

43 Seamer Lane (now Seamer Road) in 1898 reveals a mud lane, in stark contrast to the busy main road of today. The cabmen are watching a football match on the Athletic Ground which the Football Club leased from the Corporation in 1897 for 14 years. It is still going strong today.

44 The foundation stone for the Cliff Bridge was laid on 29 November 1826. At a cost of £9,000 the elegant bridge was opened on 19 July 1827. During the ceremony, and with flags waving, a Royal Mail coach galloped at full speed over the bridge. Many a genteel lady had to recover from the shock with a little lavender water. The picture was taken in 1899.

45 The Valley Bridge owes its existence to Robert Williamson, who bought the skeleton of an iron bridge which had collapsed at York, and erected it here in 1865. The view from Ramshill Road shows the completed bridge.

46 In 1891 the Valley Bridge was taken over by the Scarborough Corporation and the tolls were abolished in 1919. It was considered too narrow and plans went ahead in 1925 to widen the bridge. It took three years to complete and was opened with civic splendour by Mrs. Wilfred Ashley, wife of the Minister of Transport, on 26 July 1928.

47 A selection of horse-drawn cabs stand in Lower Prospect Road, *c.*1899. The first cab to be seen in Scarborough was in 1836. Within 60 years the number had risen to over 200 landaus and hansoms. The attraction of the season was the jockey carriage with the drivers dressed in silk blouses and racing colours.

48 A coach and four makes its way along St Nicholas Cliff, c.1899. The *Grand Hotel* can just be seen on the right. The house to the left is now demolished and the site has become the Sunken Garden.

49 A private cab trundles along Scalby Road past Foxton's Farm, c.1890. The farm was demolished in the 1960s and Wilkinson Flats now occupy the site.

50 Foxton's Mews, *c*.1896, was situated in Vine Street and is now used as a garage. W. Foxton and Son ran a livery stable, and acted as posting and job masters, hay, straw and corn merchants, and contractors for the army. They also ran drives to the country in horse-drawn charabancs; return fare two shillings (10 pence).

51 Workmen are seen here laying the tramlines for the Scarborough Electric Tram-way Company at the Aquarium Top in 1904. The first tram ran that year but it was never a very popular form of transport. The first tram to run in Scarborough was on 6 May 1904 and the last tram ran on 30 September 1931; they were succeeded by the United Automobile Services.

52 A tram passes the *New Inn* in Falsgrave, *c.*1907. Hopper and Mason's store, which was situated in Westborough until well into the 1960s, is advertised on the tram's side.

53 A tramcar makes its way past the Railway Station in 1923. The gentleman in uniform is tram inspector Robert Birley, who also changed the points when the need arose.

54   Horse-drawn and motorised vehicles competing for trade in Westborough in 1905. The Londesborough Theatre, seen in the centre of the picture, was built in 1871 but demolished in 1960. Next door is Sinfield's Confectioners with its famous logo—'All Roads Lead to Sinfield's'. Rowntree's department store, to the left, was demolished in 1990 after standing for nearly 80 years.

55   Robinson's charabanc tours from the station forecourt were a regular feature of the town in the 1920s. The charabancs' maximum speed limit was 12 m.p.h. and they could seat 23 passengers. The picture was taken in 1926.

56 It's 'all aboard' a United Services bus in 1926 for Aberdeen Walk, St Columba's church, Peasholm Park and the North Sands. This Daimler 24-seater was built in 1920 for Abraham, Robinson and Gibbons of Scarborough and Pickering. It was licensed to the United between 1926-29.

57 As far back as 1879 the Scarborough Omnibus Company operated horse-drawn buses between Falsgrave and Castle Road and to the Esplanade and North Cliff. The first licence to run a motor bus between the South Cliff and town was issued in 1920. Here we see just one of the many services operating in the 1920s.

58 Union Jack Motors operated from their depot in Hanover Road throughout the 1920s. The buses backed into an open shop that stood next to Quarton's fruit shop. This part of Hanover Road was demolished to be replaced by the Odeon Cinema.

59 Vanmen stand with their vehicles outside the Snowdrift Laundry, Scalby Road in 1945. The two middle vans had been requisitioned by the army for the duration. The laundry was demolished in 1993 and new flats are proposed.

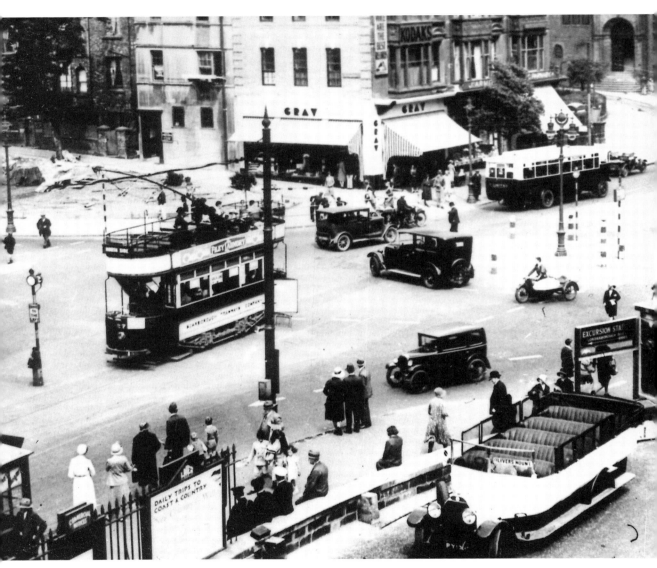

60 Westborough, looking down from the Railway Station. The year must be 1930 as Northway, on the left, is still in the process of being constructed.

61 Northway in 1955 shows a traffic-free thoroughfare in sharp contrast to the road of today. The street was constructed in 1930 after workmen bulldozed their way through Westfield Terrace, demolishing the *Westfield Hotel* and half of Albion Street. Flats were built on the open sites at each side of the road in 1960.

62 Scarborough Railway Station in 1966 when, during the last days of steam, crowds of holidaymakers are arriving. It also marked the station's decline as visitors and locals alike chose to journey by bus and car. Today, the station is only a shadow of its former self having lost a number of platforms—and porters, shunters and many other grades of men.

63 Hissing and puffing, the massive green painted steam engine, the *Flying Scotsman,* lumbered to a halt on Scarborough Station's platform on 6 April 1968. The engine carried the headboard, 'Scarborough Flyer' and crowds of sightseers willingly paid the 2s. 6d. (12½ pence) platform ticket—a rise of 2s. (10 pence)—to view this legendary engine.

Hotels and Hostelries

64 This 1882 view of Westborough, with Huntriss Row on the right, is unrecognisable today. The Bar, erected for ornamentation only by John Barry in 1847, was built to replace the original medieval structure. This too, was demolished in 1890. The *Bull Hotel* on the left became the *Balmoral Hotel*, which was also demolished 80 years later.

65 The same Bar but looking from the seaward side. North Street is on the right with the *Bar Hotel* on the corner, originally known as the *Nags Head Inn.* In time it became *The Huntsman* public house. In the 1980s it was totally gutted, by design, but retained its façade and is now a shoe shop.

66 The *Grand Hotel, c.*1890, was designed by Cuthbert Broderick. Work started on the *Cliff Hotel*, as it was originally called, in 1865, but the firm went bankrupt, a Leeds man then bought the site and the work continued. The new hotel was opened in 1867 and was said to be a 'Splendid example of Second Empire design'.

67 The *Grand Hotel* viewed in the 1890s from the South Sands, showing the Grand Hall underneath the hotel. In its time it was used as a roller skating rink, picture house and restaurant. A fire badly damaged it in 1942 and seven years later it was demolished.

68 A peaceful view of the South Sands, taken before Foreshore Road was constructed in 1874-76, shows the *Grand Hotel*, the Cliff Bridge and the elegant houses along the South Cliff. The Seawater Baths were built in 1859 and in the centre of the photograph is St Nicholas Gardens which was privately owned by the Woodall family whose home was the present Town Hall.

69 South Cliff's Esplanade, shown here in 1894, was built in the 1840s. The print captures the grandeur of the *Crown Hotel* on the right; Alga House in the centre—now called the Villa Esplanade—and on the left of the picture, at the end of the terrace, is the *Prince of Wales Hotel*. At the bottom of the picture can be seen the domes of the Spa.

70 The Esplanade and the *Prince of Wales Hotel*, seen here in 1901. The hotel was built in 1850 as a terrace of houses, before it was converted into an hotel about 1860. It closed in the late 1980s and has now been developed into luxury apartments.

71 The Cliff Lift was constructed in 1874 mainly through the efforts of Richard Hunt, the manager of the *Prince of Wales Hotel*, which can just be seen at the top of the cliff. The system worked on the principal of two tanks alternately filling and emptying with sea-water so that the trams moved up and down.

72 The elegant Esplanade, taken about 1895, shows in the background the *Crown Hotel* which opened in 1844. The first lease of the hotel was held by John Fairgrey Sharpin.

73 The *Strawberry Gardens Inn* stood at what is now the junction of Cambridge Place and Mount Park Road. It was in a dilapidated state when this photograph was taken in 1880. Nesfield, seen advertised on the board, was a local brewer who lived at Auborough House, Auborough Street.

74 The *Broadway Temperance Hotel*, 77 Westborough, in 1896, is unrecognisable today. It was opened in about 1881 by Benjamin Goodwill who ran a grocery shop from the same premises. Mr. Goodwill is seen in the doorway with one of the porters. The last proprietress was Mrs. Crossley in 1911. Shortly afterwards the building was converted into offices.

75 The *Pavilion Hotel*, Westborough was built to a design by William Baldwin Stewart in 1870 and stood majestically outside the Railway Station. It was demolished amid much controversy in 1973. A tram is making its way along the street which dates the view to about 1906.

76 Just after 1 p.m. on 12 November 1954 a fire broke out in the south turret of the *Pavilion Hotel*. Flames were soon shooting out of the roof and windows. The fire brigade was quickly on the scene and fireman Harry Abram was raised over 70 feet to direct a jet of water onto the flames which were soon extinguished.

77 The *Westlands Hotel* in 1934 stood opposite the Railway Station. At the turn of the century the building was Dr. Rooke's Warehouse. Doctors Charles and W. F. Rooke were patent medicine manufacturers. Their Pills Elixir and Oriental pills were considered a boon for the nervous and afflicted. The hotel was demolished in 1935.

78 Queen's Parade was never regarded as being quite as elegant as the South Cliff, although it possessed all the features to make it so. It catered mainly to the middle-classes, whereas South Cliff catered exclusively to the more affluent visitor. The *Norbreck Hotel*, in the centre of the picture, was built in 1850. When this photograph was taken, *c.*1900, it was known as the *Albion Hotel* and still retained its original façade.

79 The *Bee Hive Inn*, Sandside, seen here in 1897, lost its licence in 1904 after complaints by the clergy because of the noise and drunkenness. The sign above the door reads, 'Within this hive we are all alive, good ale will make you funny, if you are dry as you pass by, step in and taste our honey'.

80 Sandside, *c*.1902, and the towering battlements of the castle look down on a scene very different from today's amusement arcades and ice-cream parlours. The white-coloured building on the left is the *Lancaster Inn* which opened in 1875. The adjoining properties, the *Dog and Duck Inn* and the *Shipwright's Arms*, were incorporated into the new building.

81 The *Lancaster Inn*, Sandside, was established by William Lancaster in 1875. He converted the adjoining properties and incorporated them in the new pub.

82 The *Queen's Hotel*, built in the 1850s on North Marine Road, was requisitioned by the military at the beginning of the Second World War. The troops caused so much damage that this and the damage caused by a bomb which exploded opposite on 18 March 1941 persuaded the Corporation to order its demolition in 1946.

'Queen of the Yorkshire Coast'

83 Taken from the Esplanade in 1890, this scene depicts the stark contrast between the affluent Spa in the foreground and the old town lying below the Castle. The observation tower in the foreground was built by Sir Joseph Paxton in about 1860 and was demolished in 1923.

84 The view from the Old Pier in 1894 shows the fine sweep of the South Bay and the imposing façade of the *Grand Hotel*. A manuscript written in the reign of Henry III states that he granted a patent 'for making a new pier at Scardeburgh with timber and stone towards the sea'.

85 The 'Church Parade' along the Esplanade was one of those strange customs that ceased with the outbreak of the First World War. Ladies and gentlemen of refinement, dressed in their Sunday best, would promenade up and down the street nodding genteely to acquaintances. A parasol was definitely *de rigueur*.

86 Peasholm Gap in 1870, upper right. There is no Marine Drive—only the North Pier, the bathing huts and the donkeys. The Corner Café, which now stands where the bathing huts were situated, was officially opened on 29 June 1925.

87 The photograph on the right, taken in 1874 at Peasholm Gap, shows one of Brown's bathing huts. These huts first appeared around 1735 and by the early 19th century there were 30 to 40 on the south beach alone. It was said that bathing on the sands caused great excitement and pleasure to the promenaders.

88 This 1897 view of the Northside, (left) looking towards Castle Hill, shows the Royal Albert Drive, built in 1890, and the pier still intact—it was destroyed in a storm in 1905. The Corner Café, which today occupies the site where the bathing huts are sited in the picture, was not built until the latter half of 1924, and officially opened the following year.

89 The North Bay Pier (right) was built to a design by Mr. Eugene Birch at a cost of £6,000 in 1869. It was not popular and even after Quinton Gibson, a local entertainer, built the pavilion at the seaward end it proved a failure. The pier was washed away in a storm on 7 January 1905.

90 Flagstaff Hill in Clarence Gardens was laid out in 1890 to honour the visit of Prince Albert, Duke of Clarence, who opened the Royal Albert Drive. It was flattened in the early part of the present century and the bandstand was moved into Falsgrave Park, where it remained until about 1930.

91 Warwick's revolving tower was erected on the North Cliff in 1898. A lift carried sightseers up to the revolving tower. It was considered an eyesore, especially by a Mr. Shuttleworth who lived on the South Cliff. Using his own money, he paid for the tower to be dismantled in 1907.

92 This quiet and secluded stretch of beach near the Spa was, and still is, known as Children's Corner. The photograph, taken in 1900, shows only a few people paddling in the sea; the custom then was to use the bathing huts which can be seen in the distance.

93 A trip in a rowing boat in the South Bay at the turn of the century was considered most daring by the fairer sex.

94 Victorian ladies brave the salt spray, which must have been unkind to their soft, lily-white complexions, to watch the passing sails in the South Bay.

95 Viewed from St Nicholas Gardens at the turn of the century, the South Bay is seen at its best. A large fleet of herring boats lies at anchor, whilst a pleasure steamer slowly sails by. Two more are moored to the Lighthouse Pier. Note the pebble stalls on the sands.

96 Looking across the South Bay in 1920. With a view such as this it was hardly surprising that Scarborough was honoured with the title, 'Queen of the Yorkshire Coast'.

97 Unlike the previous picture, the sands are almost deserted and little can be seen in the way of development, but the 'Queen' still presents a majestic quality. The North 'Orchestra', as bandstands were then known, was constructed over the Pump Room at the Spa in 1874. After it ceased to be used for music, in 1910 it was converted into a room for the public to enjoy the spa water. It was demolished in 1931.

War and the Military

98 Officers of the Scarborough Rifle Volunteers, formed in the late 18th century, pose in the grounds of St Nicholas House in 1861. John Woodall, the owner of the house and also the regiment's major, stands on the balcony. Today, the house is the Town Hall.

99 During the First World War 'Sister Susie' may have 'sewed shirts for soldiers', but here the local fisherfolk under the supervision of the stalwart Miss Barker of South Cliff make sandbags for the front. They are seen in 1914 outside the Seamen's Institute, Sandside.

100 On 16 December 1914, German warships bombarded Scarborough. Their first target was the Signal Station in the Castle grounds. Those on duty are pictured here: *back row, from left to right*, A. Dean, James Walsh, L. Reeve, Robert Barnes, P. C. H. Hunter and James Eastwood; *front row, left to right*, Wilfred Durant, George Mason and Harry Holden.

101 During the same bombardment, Mr. Charles Herbert's house at 79 Commercial Street took a direct hit. It was some seven hours after the raid that a woman in her eighties and her daughter were found in an upstairs room. In 1941 the house suffered another direct hit when a heavy bomb landed on it.

102 Mrs. Emily Merryweather, aged 80 of 43 Prospect Road, opened her door in an act of kindness to admit two frightened ladies who were caught in the raid. As she opened the door a shell exploded in front of the house killing her instantly. The property was demolished in 1987 and rebuilt as a private house and shop.

103 The elegant Georgian houses along St Nicholas Parade received direct hits from the German 12-inch guns during the raid.

104 One of the last shots fired in the raid by German warships hit 2 Wykeham Street. It killed four out of the seven occupants and completely destroyed the house.

105 The funeral procession of the victims who were killed in Wykeham Street during the bombardment winds its way along Dean Road to the cemetery, accompanied by soldiers of the 5th Yorkshire Regiment.

106 The last shot of the bombardment was fired about 8.30 a.m. and passed straight through the lighthouse tower. The damage was extensive resulting in the tower having to be demolished. It was 1931 before a new tower was built, paid for by funds raised by the Townmen's Association.

107 Wounded soldiers convalescing at the Royal Sea Bathing Infirmary on the Foreshore were quickly carried downstairs by the nurses only seconds before a shell burst in the ward.

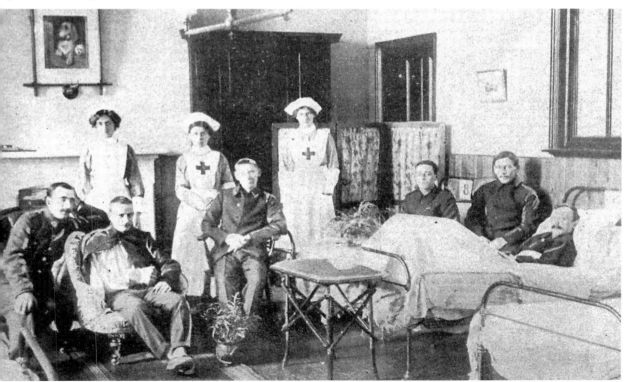

108 The barracks in the castle grounds were destroyed in the raid. The last troops to occupy them left in 1878. At the time of the bombardment the building was in use as a store.

109 Soldiers who had been rushed to Scarborough from York after the bombardment stand guard outside the ruins of Kingscliff Holiday Camp on King Street.

110 The bright uniforms of the local 'Terriers'—the 5th Yorkshire Regiment—stir the patriotic feelings of the spectators as they march down Castle Road in 1915 in a church parade held in conjunction with the Scarborough Company of the National Reserve.

111 With the *Pavilion Hotel* in the background, local lads of the 5th Yorkshire R.F.A. march towards the Railway Station in 1915 en route for Darlington where they were to train before being sent to the front. For many it would be a final goodbye to Scarborough.

112 On 17 March 1915 the Scarborough 'Pals' Battery was formed. Its official name was 'C' Battery, 161st (Yorkshire) Brigade, R.F.A. Posing against the Castle Keep are a number of officers and men of the unit. Lieut. T. Kay (Commanding Officer) is seen, seated third from the right.

113 It was just after 9 p.m. on 10 October 1940 when a landmine exploded in Potter Lane causing the damage seen in this photograph. Four people died under the rubble of Potter Lane, Anderson Terrace and Short's Gardens. After rebuilding, Potter Lane was renamed Castle Gardens.

114 On 18 March 1941, in the heaviest air raid the town had witnessed, 98 enemy planes dropped thousands of incendiaries and high explosives for over two hours. The printing firm of E. T. W. Dennis and Sons in Melrose Street was hit and soon ablaze. Firemen fought the fire even while the bombs rained down on them, but despite their valiant efforts the building was gutted.

115 This terrace of houses in Commercial Street suffered a direct hit during the height of the raid on 18 March 1941, resulting in the death of seven people. Pre-fabricated buildings were erected after the war and are still there today.

116 Scarborough was divided into sections each with its own A.R.P. unit. Here we see the personnel of the Grange Avenue A.R.P. outside their headquarters at 3 Grange Avenue in 1941.

Religion

117 St Martin's-on-the-Hill, *c*.1868. The church was built from a donation of £10,000 by Mary Craven, the daughter of Robert Martin Craven, a Hull surgeon, to a design by George Frederick Bodley, and opened in 1863. Miss Craven died in a house on the Esplanade in 1889 at 75 years of age.

118 St Martin's-on-the-Hill in 1896. The church is enriched by the works of the leading Pre-Raphaelite artists Dante Gabriel Rossetti, Edward Burne-Jones, Ford Maddox Brown and many lesser mortals.

119 St Mary's church and the picturesque Castle Road with Rutland Terrace on the left. This view was taken in 1899 and shows a street as yet untouched by the holiday trade. The writing on the van reads, 'Dry rooms for storage, Army Contractors'. The parish church on the right dates from about 1148 with later additions.

120 Taken in 1901 this view shows Church Stairs Street leading up to St Mary's church. It was here that John Wesley, the founder of Wesleyan Methodism, preached at the newly-erected church in 1772. In the early 1950s the street had not changed in character but today both the church and the street have been demolished.

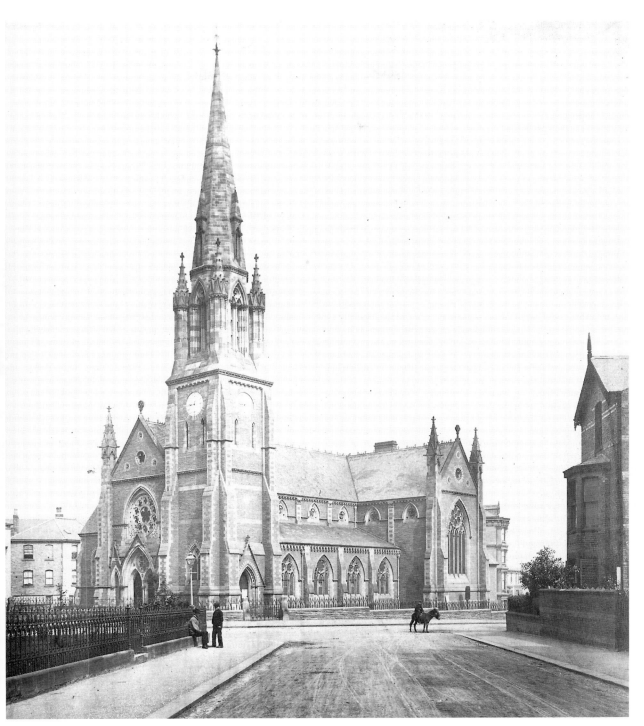

121 The South Cliff Congregational church on Ramshill Road is known by locals as Balgarnie's church. The Rev. Robert Balgarnie became minister of this church when it opened in 1865.

122 Ramshill Road, *c.*1900 and Balgarnie's church. The Rev. Robert Balgarnie was minister of the Bar Church in 1851 and, when the town expanded outwards, Sir Titus Salt was responsible for the church in Ramshill Road being built.

123 Bar church, at the junction of Westborough and Aberdeen Walk, *c.*1905. The site was purchased for £900 and the foundation stone laid on 5 February 1850 by Lady Lowthorpe. The architect was Raffles Brown, the nephew of Dr. Raffles of Liverpool. It was demolished in the late 1960s and a night club now occupies the site.

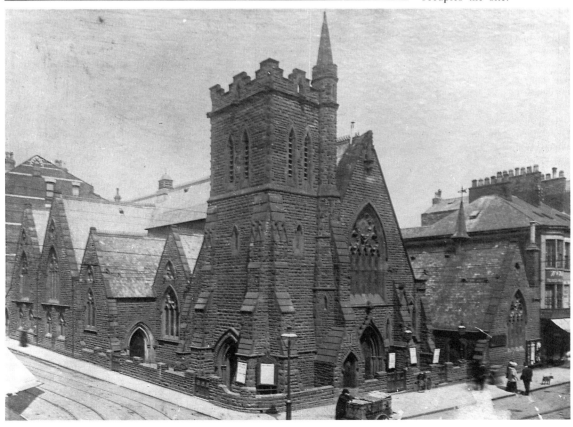

Public Services

124 Scarborough Hospital and Dispensary, Friars Entry, was built to a design by Frank Tugwell and opened in 1893 on the site of the demolished Wesleyan Day School. When the hospital in Scalby Road was built in 1934-6, the old Hospital took second place, closing shortly afterwards. It has since been demolished and a car park now covers the area.

125 The Cottage Hospital, Springhill Road, was founded in 1871 by Mrs. Anne Wright, widow of a Birmingham surgeon. It did excellent work but social and economic changes forced it to close in 1931. The Anne Wright Ward at Scarborough Hospital was named in recognition of her work. The old Cottage Hospital was converted into flats which remain to this day.

126 The Old Township school, 1870, was built in 1804. It stood roughly where the first house of Mount Park Road is situated. John Cross of Sandybed Farm (now Lisvane school) contributed 10 guineas toward the building of the school and a sum of £6 15s. 0d. was donated by Mr. Richard Sawdon to 'buy a bell for the school'. The establishment became redundant with the building of the Falsgrave school in 1873.

127 Nelson House, 4 Filey Road, was built in the 1860s as a private house. In the 1890s it was converted by Arthur Butler Brockwood into a private school for boys. The fees ranged from 10 guineas (£10.50) for day scholars to £26 for boarders per year. Today, the house has been converted into flats.

128 Stately-looking Valley Bridge House, 6 Ramshill Road, was a high-class school for girls run by the principals, Mrs. and Miss Winter. It was said to be the best establishment, situated as it was in the healthiest part of the town. Pupils from India and the Colonies were accepted.

129 Pupils of Falsgrave school, which opened in 1873, pose for this photograph taken just after the turn of the century.

130 Roseberry preparatory school, 15 Fulford Road, in 1904. Osbert Sitwell, whose family owned the present Woodend Museum, is seated third from the left. The principal, Mr. William Sanderson, is standing in the back row.

131 Miss Mary Craven, as well as donating £10,000 for St Martin's church, also gave money for the building of St Martin's grammar school at 60 Ramshill Road, shown here in 1923. Bodley was again the architect and the establishment opened in 1870. In the 1960s half the building was demolished; the other half is now being used as a café.

132 This photograph taken in 1913 shows the fire brigade with their first motor fire engine which had been a gift to the service the previous year by Gambart Baines. It was equipped with a 50-ft. Ajax Escape and a 500-gallons-per-minute centrifugal-type pump. Until then the brigade had used a horse-drawn Shand Mason steam fire engine. Ernest Gambart Baines of 42 Aberdeen Walk had moved to Scarborough in 1902 and had become a property owner and owner of the Salt Water Baths on the Foreshore. He became a keen bowler and in 1919 presented the first Gambart Baines Trophy—a cup still played for to this day.

133 Members of the Auxiliary Fire Service stand with their fire engine in 1942.

134 The Town Hall in 1928. It was originally called St Nicholas House and was built in 1844 for John Woodall. In 1898 the Corporation bought the property and a new wing was added in 1903. Further extensions were built between 1962-4.

135 On 24 July 1942 Ye Olde Booke Stall was set up outside the Town Hall in a salvage book drive. The Deputy Mayor is seen next to Johnny Jackson, one-time mayor of Scarborough. Over 160 tons of books were collected.

136   The Oddfellows' Hall, Vernon Road was built in 1840. The architects were J. Gibson and W. Johnson. It was altered by John Hall in 1862 and became the Mechanics' Institute. The Corporation decided to reconstruct the building and it was formally opened by Sir Meredith Whittaker on 19 June 1930 as the public library.

Leisure and Entertainment

137 Promenading on the Spa in 1893 was considered the correct thing to do for the upper classes.

138 The famous Will Catlin's Pierrots in 1897. They were formed in 1896 to entertain the holiday-makers on the South Sands. Note the parasols for the ladies—a sun tan was then considered terribly vulgar.

139 One of the main attractions of the seaside was the donkey rides. The majestic *Grand Hotel* stands to the left, and the Seawater Baths, Foreshore Road, now an amusement arcade, is to the right. The photograph was taken before 1893 because the Exhibition Building, designed by J. Caleb Petch, which later became the Olympia, had not then been built.

140 Vasey's donkeys on the South Sands slipway in 1902. There were many donkey families plying their trades on the sands, including 'Donkey' Elliot and the Kings.

141 Plans went ahead to erect baths in Ramshill Road in 1875. The architect was John Petch. The South Cliff Bath Co. Ltd. opened their premises the following year. Every bath from warm and cold seawater, electro-chemical and Dialytic to magnetic, galvanic and ozone was available. During the present century the building became a garage but· has since been demolished.

142 The Seawater Baths were built in 1859 and were fed by a pipe which ran directly from the sea. This photograph of the baths was taken in 1896. The baths were sold in 1920. Bath Terrace, to the left, is now demolished.

143 On 18 July 1903 the Kiralphi brothers opened up their new Arcadia on the foreshore. The visitors were delighted at the Mountain Railway and Fairy River. Catlin then purchased it in 1909 before demolishing it to build his own Arcadia. The building on the right is a cabman's shelter. Today, the Futurist Theatre occupies the site.

144 A bandstand was built over the Spa Pump Room in 1875 but visitors could still take the waters by descending the stone steps and dipping cups into the well. The service was abolished in 1890 for the more hygienic method of bottled water. The bandstand was demolished in 1931 and the well was blocked off. A kiosk stood on the site until 1980 when it too was demolished.

145 The Spa Band in 1911. As far back as 1837 a local band played on the Spa during the summer season for which they were payed £10 10s. 0d. Receipts showed the company how popular this kind of entertainment was and Kohler's Band was engaged. The years 1867-79 saw Pritchard's Band on the Spa, followed in the years 1884-92 by Meyer Lutz's Band. In 1912 Alick Maclean began his long association with the Spa.

146 The Floral Hall was built in the Alexandra Gardens in 1910. It became the 'home' of the Fol-de-Rols which George Royle formed in 1911. Many of its performers—Arthur Askey, Reg Dixon and Jack Warner—have become household names. The Floral Hall was demolished in 1987.

147 The Floral Hall was the home of the Fol-de-Rols where they entertained from 1911, with only a short break, until well into the 1960s before they were disbanded.

148 It's 'take your partners for the one-step' in the glass-covered walkway above the Spa Grand Hall. The year was 1912 and it is a puzzle as to where the dancers performed this lively dance.

149 The Spa toll booths at the entrance to the Cliff Bridge, *c*.1920. In 1951 the Scarborough Corporation purchased the bridge and, after abolishing the tolls, demolished the toll booths the following year.

150 The 'Butterfly Queen' was staged by members of the Gladstone Road chapel in 1926. The Rev. Goldsborough is seen far right next to Mrs. Dobson, whose face can be seen just peeping out. Miss Gough is seen on the left in a checked dress; Frances Pottage second from left in the back row is a bluebell and Harold Kew is wearing a top hat.

151 Peasholm Glen, seen here in 1935, was originally called Wilson's Wood before it was landscaped by Harry W. Smith, the borough engineer, and opened to the public in 1924. It made a pleasant route from Peasholm Park which had been created by Mr. Smith in 1912.

152 The British Tunny Club was formed in Scarborough in 1932. This view shows the club's headquarters at 1 East Sandgate which was originally the *Victoria Inn*. The house is still there today, but is now a café.

153 The Town Clerk, Mr. E. C. Horsfall-Turner, proudly poses with the tunny he caught on 24 August 1949. The fish weighed 582 lb. and was caught from the *Shirley Williamson* skippered by Ernie Williamson.

154 The staff of the Clock Tower Café seen here in 1914, the year after it was built in the Spa gardens. Slightly above it was an open piece of ground on which an old cottage stood, but this was subsequently demolished. It was the home of Jarvis the Quaker who sold flowers in the town—'Who'll buy my beauties?'.

155 The Olympia restaurant above the dance hall was a haven for soldiers during the war. The building burnt down in 1975 and the site remained undeveloped until an amusement arcade was built in the 1980s.

156 The Grand Restaurant on Foreshore Road was built in 1865. Extensions were added in 1876. It has been used for many purposes including roller skating and a picture house. The army occupied it during the war until a fire broke out in 1942. It was demolished in 1949.

157 The People's Palace and Aquarium was designed by Eugenius Birch (1818-84), the architect responsible for the Brighton Palace and pier. Costing over £100,000 and covering three acres, the new underground attraction was opened in 1875. This view taken in 1952 shows the Aquarium Top looking over to the disused swimming baths.

158 The good ship *Hispaniola* arrives in Scarborough by road in June 1949. It was constructed in Hull by Don Nelson to a design by B. Lawrenson. The 46-footer, rigged as a three-masted brigantine, was the brainchild of George Horrocks, the Scarborough Corporation entertainments manager.

159 With the Jolly Roger flying, the *Hispaniola* sets sail on her maiden voyage on the Mere, 18 June 1949. The mayor and his party had gone to the island in a motor boat but on the trip back the ship broke down and His Worship had to be taken off to lighten the load as the *Hispaniola* grounded.

160 Long John Silver (Tom Hunt) and Jim Hawkins (Harry Moore) and another old salt inspect the ship before she sets sail for Treasure Island.

161 Foreshore Road in 1953. In the background is the summer attraction of the year, the spaceship 'Anastasia', christened by the film star Frances Day on Whit Monday, 1953. Until it was sold in 1954 and dismantled the following year, a trip to the moon, via a television screen, became a reality for hundreds of children and adults.

162 The murky depths of Galaland, nicknamed the 'Scarborough Umbrella', were a delight to young and old alike. Over 5,000 people could be accommodated in this amusement arcade. It started life as the Peoples' Palace and Aquarium in 1877 with Mr. McMillan, director of the Brighton Aquarium, as the prime mover. The Corporation took it over in 1921 and demolished it c.1968.

163 Thelma Hammond and her all-girl orchestra, pictured here in the Galaland theatre, were a popular attraction throughout the early 1950s.

164 Peaceful and idyllic Scalby Mills with the bubbling Scalby Beck and its stepping stones is now a thing of the past. When this photograph was taken in 1959 it would have been unthinkable that a beauty spot would cause, some thirty years later, so much controversy through the building of a sewerage works.

People and Events

165   John Woodall (above left) was a member of a prominent Scarborough banking family. The bank itself, Bell, Woodall and Company, stood at the corner of St Nicholas Street in 1864. In 1896 Barclay's Bank took over the site. John Woodall died on 9 February 1879 and it was his son, John Woodall Woodall, who offered St Nicholas House to the Corporation.

166   William Tindall of the Scarborough banking and shipbuilding family is seen (above right) as a rather portly gentleman. He was also brave, as became evident when he was swept to his death along with Lord Charles Beauclerc and another person whilst trying to secure ropes onto the schooner *Coupland* as she was dashed against the Spa wall during a storm in 1861.

167   John Fairgrey Sharpin J.P. (below left) was born in Ripon and was educated in the wine and spirit trade in London. After the lease on the *Crown* expired in 1851, he purchased a plot of land in Huntriss Row and built the Assembly Rooms which opened in 1857. Sharpin was the youngest mayor in England when he was elected in Scarborough at the age of 32 in 1853.

168   Robert Cattle, Sheriff of York (below right), was the man mainly responsible for establishing the Cliff Bridge Company, which officially came into being at a meeting in the *George Hotel*, York. Stead, Snowden and Buckley of York and Hird and Co. of Bradford were engaged on the stone and iron work for the new bridge.

169 Residents of the old town had been solidly behind Sir George Sitwell right up until the election on 16 July 1895, but he finally lost to Joseph Rickett, the Liberal candidate. Tindall's Lane, which runs from Sandside to Quay Street, can just be made out on a street sign, and is the only clue as to where this view was taken.

170 'Vote for Rickett, Equal treatment for rich and poor' reads the poster urging people to vote for the Liberal candidate Joseph Compton Rickett. The propaganda worked because he defeated Sir George Sitwell by 24 votes in the election held on 16 July 1895. The fire station was built on the site of the shop to the rear.

171 The Scarborough Phoo Phoo Band was formed by local tradesmen. They performed at various venues around the town to raise money for charity. The photograph was taken about 1894 outside Ellicker's tinsmith shop in Sussex Street, which stood opposite Brogden and Wilson. Ellicker is seen seated with concertina and J. S. Downham, photographer, is on his right with the banjo.

172 Mr. Kneale Kelly (right) became director of music at the Spa from 1936-39 and 1945-49. He replaced Alexander Morvaren Maclean, who had reigned from 1912. The other gentleman is Mr. Fred Hastings, manager of the Spa, who replaced the ex-manager of the Futurist Theatre, Will Emmerson, who died in 1928.

173 A circus procession winds its way down Prospect Road, possibly in 1904 as the tramlines have not been laid.

174 Officers and men of the Channel Fleet march up Newborough, having received the freedom of the town, on 27 July 1906. The properties opposite, which included the businesses of Bean and Sons, Hurst's and Lord's, stood between St Helen's Square and Queen Street, but were demolished in 1964 to make way for a bowling alley.

175 The South Bay pool was opened in 1915 and improvements were made after the Armistice of 1918. Here we see what may be the opening ceremony, as there are one or two men in army uniform, which points to it being taken during the First World War.

176 On 5 August 1932, the Lord Mayor of London, Sir Maurice Jenks, and other dignitaries arrived in state to attend the opening of the Open Air Theatre and also to declare the Glen Bridge open. In pouring rain spectators watched the civic coaches arrive at the junction of Glen Side and North Leas Avenue.

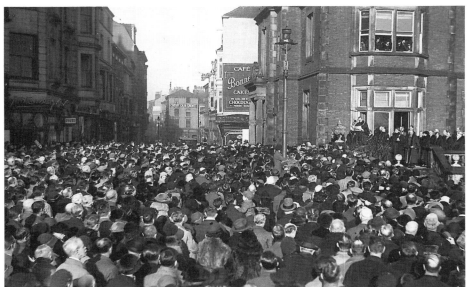

177 A crowd is gathered in St Nicholas Street outside the Town Hall to hear the mayor read the Proclamation of King George VI in 1936. Bonnet's famous chocolate shop can be seen in the background. The building was demolished in 1963 to make way for the Town Hall extensions.

178 To celebrate V.E. Day on 8 May 1945 street parties were held throughout the town. Here we see the residents of Middle Walk enjoying the festivities.

179 In pouring rain on Sunday, 13 May 1945, crowds gathered in Westborough outside the Railway Station as 3,000 members of the armed forces took part in a thanksgiving service to celebrate the defeat of Germany and the end of the war.

180 On Friday, 26 October 1945 the Freedom of the Borough was conferred upon the 5th Battalion, the Green Howards. This allowed them the privilege of marching through the streets of Scarborough with fixed bayonets, drums beating and colours flying. The Mayor, Alderman G. Pindar, takes the salute.

181 The Mayor, Councillor J. W. Hardcastle, dressed in his robes of office and surrounded by other members of the Corporation, reads the Proclamation of Queen Elizabeth II in February 1952, in the Town Hall gardens.

Lord Londes... Louis B.Palm... Boehricka... Sir Charles Rigne... E. Wood... all... ...der

Phil May '00